Under the Sea
تحت البحر

يَا تُرَى، مَاذَا تَرَى تَحْتَ البَحْرِ؟

I see a fish smiling at me!

يَا تُرَى، مَاذَا تَرَى تَحْتَ البَحْرِ؟

I see a starfish winking at me!

أَنَا أَرَى نَجْمَةَ البَحْرِ تَغْمِزُ لِي !

يَا تُرَى، مَاذَا تَرَى تَحْتَ البَحْرِ؟

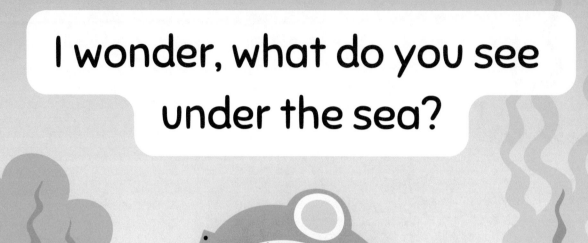

يَا تُرَى، مَاذَا تَرَى تَحْتَ البَحْرِ؟

يَا تُرَى، مَاذَا تَرَى تَحْتَ البَحْرِ؟

I see a dolphin throwing a ball at me!

أَنَا أَرَى دِلْفِينًا يَرْمِي الكُرَةَ لِي !

I wonder, what do you see under the sea?

يَا تُرَى، مَاذَا تَرَى تَحْتَ البَحْرِ؟

يَا تُرَى، مَاذَا تَرَى تَحْتَ البَحْرِ؟

I see a crab angry at me!

أَنَا أَرَى سَلْطَعُونًا غَاضِبًا مِنِّي !

يَا تُرَى، مَاذَا تَرَى تَحْتَ البَحْرِ؟

I see a **shark** singing for me!

We wonder, what do you see under the sea?

يَا تُرَى، مَاذَا تَرَى تَحْتَ البَحْرِ؟

نَحْنُ نَرَى قِنْديلَ البَحْرِ غَارِقًا فِي نَوْمِهِ!

Fish
سمكة

Starfish
نجمة البحر

Dolphin
دلفين

Crab
سلطعون

Sea Turtle
سلحفاة البحر

Octopus
أخطبوط

Seal
فقمة

Shark
قرش

Jellyfish
قنديل البحر

Made in United States
Cleveland, OH
26 November 2024

10980563R00024